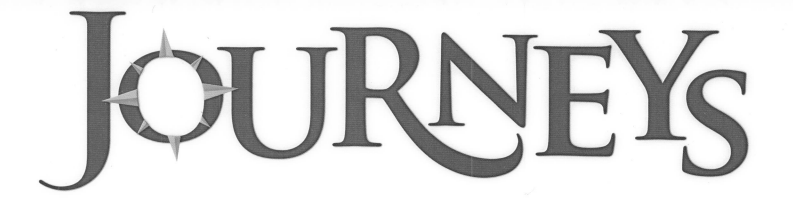

# JOURNEYS

# Ready-Made Work Stations

## Independent Activities

# Think and Write

GRADE
3

HOUGHTON MIFFLIN HARCOURT
School Publishers

ART CREDITS
Unit 1: Week 2 (1) John Haslam. Week 3 (1) Tracey Wood. Week 5 (1) John Haslam. Unit 2: Week 2 (1) Tim Haggerty. Week 3 (1) Chris Reed. Week 5 (2) Tim Haggerty. Unit 3: Week 2 (2) Andy Levine. Week 3 (1) Chris Reed. Unit 4: Week 1 (1) Tim Haggerty. Week 3 (1) Tim Haggerty. Week 4 (1) Dave Klug. (2) John Haslam. Week 5 (1) John Haslam. Unit 5: Week 1 (2) John Haslam. Week 2 (1) John Haslam. Week 5 (1) John Haslam.

PHOTOGRAPHY
All photographs © Houghton Mifflin Harcourt Publishers, except as noted below.

Unit 1: Week 3 (2) Leland Bobbe/Getty Images. Unit 2: Week 1 (2) © Michel Touraine/pixland/Corbis. Week 3 (2) Houghton Mifflin Harcourt Publishers. Week 4 (1) Corbis (RF)/Jupiter Images. (2) Photodisc/Alamy. Unit 3: Week 1 (2) © Reuters/Corbis. Week 2 (1) Workbook Stock/Jupiter Images. Week 3 (2) © Burstein Collection/Corbis. Week 4 (1) Dale C. Spartas/Corbis. (2) Martin Harvey/Gallo Images/Corbis. Week 5 (2) © Photo Network/Alamy. Unit 4: Week 2 (1) Oxford Scientific/Jupiter Images. (2) © Bettmann/Corbis. Week 5 (2) Comstock Images/Jupiter Images. Unit 5: Week 2 (2) Visual&Written SL/Alamy. Week 4 (1) David Deas/Getty Images. (2) David Fleetham/Alamy. Week 5 (2) © Galen Rowell/Corbis.

Printed in China

ISBN 10: 0-54-712590-9
ISBN 13: 978-0-54-712590-9

7 8 9-0940-14 13 12

4500353062

HOUGHTON MIFFLIN HARCOURT
School Publishers

# Think and Write

# Contents

## Unit 1

Lesson 1:  Which School?
Lesson 2:  Words in Court!
Lesson 3:  Help Your Community
Lesson 4:  Where We Live
Lesson 5:  Interview a Classmate

## Unit 2

Lesson 6:  Give Me Directions
Lesson 7:  Make a Book!
Lesson 8:  Making Things Happen
Lesson 9:  Read and Respond
Lesson 10:  Modern Inventions

## Unit 3

Lesson 11:  A Journal Entry
Lesson 12:  Great Ideas
Lesson 13:  Great Chiefs and Leaders
Lesson 14:  A Helpful Partner
Lesson 15:  You're the Chef!

## Unit 4

Lesson 16:  Save the Rainforests!
Lesson 17:  Report-a-saurus
Lesson 18:  Did You Know?
Lesson 19:  Dogzilla: The Next Chapter
Lesson 20:  It's Cold Outside!

## Unit 5

Lesson 21:  Write a Report
Lesson 22:  On Their Way
Lesson 23:  Time for a Journey
Lesson 24:  Exercise for Good Health
Lesson 25:  Interview an Explorer

# Reach Higher!

## My School Is Great!

- Choose one of the great things about your school and write a thank-you note to a person who helps make that part of your school so great.

- Make sure that you include the date, greeting, body, closing, and signature.

- Include two or three sentences that tell why you think something in your school is great. Check each sentence to be sure it includes a subject and predicate.

- Share your letter with a partner.

# Challenge Yourself!

## Comparing Schools

- Reread *One-Room Schoolhouses*. Write a paragraph comparing the one-room schoolhouse with your school.

- What are the advantages of being in a classroom with students in different grades? How have schools changed today? In your opinion, are schools today better or not as good? Explain why.

- Check your writing for grammar and spelling errors. Be sure to indent your paragraph. Share your writing with a partner.

# Which School?

**You will need:**
Student Book,
paper,
pencil or pen

## Get Started!

1. Think about *A Fine, Fine School*. Now think about your own school. How are the schools the same? How are they different?

2. Write a paragraph to compare the two schools. What did you like about Mr. Keene's school? What do you like about your school? What would you keep the same? What would you change?

3. Read your paragraph to a group of classmates. Do they agree or disagree with your ideas?

You will need:

Student Book,
Reading Log,
reference books,
paper,
pencil or pen,
crayons or markers

# Reach Higher!

## Guilty or Not Guilty?

- Use the vocabulary words from the Get Started! activity.

- Use your Reading Log to record the events of the trial that took place in *The Trial of Cardigan Jones*.

- Pretend you are a member of the jury. Using the events that took place in the story, write a response. How did the townspeople and judge treat Cardigan? What would you have done as a juror?

- Share your response with your partner and other classmates.

# Challenge Yourself!

## Make a Brochure

- The Supreme Court is the highest court in our nation. With a partner, find information about the Supreme Court. Use reference books to help you.

- Make a brochure that teaches others about the Supreme Court.

- Share your brochure with your class.

 # Words in Court!

**You will need:**

Student Book,
Vocabulary Log,
dictionary,
paper,
pencil or pen

## Get Started!

1. With a partner, review *The Trial of Cardigan Jones*.

2. Make a list of words in the story that relate to the justice system or trials, such as *arrested*, *jury*, *witnesses*, and *the stand*.

3. Look up the meanings of these words. Write the words and their meanings in your Vocabulary Log.

4. Share your words with other partners. Add to your list the words you did not find.

# Reach Higher!

**You will need:**

local newspaper,
paper,
pencil or pen,
crayons or markers

## Working Together

- Think about a problem that you once had that required others to help you. Think about how you solved the problem with the help you received.

- Make a story map, including the problem, the solution, and the steps you took to solve your problem.

- Write a personal narrative about your problem and how it was solved. Proofread your work and correct any sentence fragments.

- Draw a picture to go with your paragraph. Display your work in the classroom.

# Challenge Yourself!

## Solve a Problem

- In a small group, read the headlines of a local newspaper. Look for a story about people in a community solving a problem together.

- Take turns reading the article aloud. Make an outline of the events and the problem and solution.

- Write a paragraph about the problem and solution. How did solving this problem help the community? Could the problem have been solved in another way? Tell about it. Read your paragraph to another classmate.

# Help Your Community

**You will need:**

Student Book,
paper,
pencil or pen

## Get Started!

1. Think about the things Destiny and the community did to help Mrs. Wade in *Destiny's Gift*.

2. Do you think the bookstore will remain open or will it close? Why do you think so? Would you have helped Mrs. Wade? What would you have done?

3. Write a response to the story. Tell what you would do and the steps you would take. Explain how your plan could be successful.

4. Read your response to another classmate. Does the classmate agree or disagree? Ask him or her to explain why.

# Reach Higher!

## The Law Rules!

- Think about how the rules that you follow in your school help students work together. With a partner, discuss why rules are important and how they help students work together. List the rules.

- With a partner, brainstorm the rules and laws in your community. List the laws you know about that help citizens work together.

- With your partner, list three new rules that you think students in your school and citizens in your community should follow to help them work together. Share your rules with other partners.

# Challenge Yourself!

## Go, Team!

- Think about a job in your school or community where people can work together, such as cleaning up the playground, recycling, or putting on a play.

- Write a plan to get the project done. List the jobs that would be needed to complete the project. List the steps in the order they should be done.

- If time permits, tell the class how working together can make your project work.

# Where We Live

**You will need:**

Student Book,
paper,
pencil or pen

## Get Started!

1. The story *Pop's Bridge* takes place in San Francisco. What can you tell about San Francisco's physical features from the selection? Describe the setting of this story. Then describe the physical features of where you live.

2. Write a paragraph comparing San Francisco to the city or town you live in. Share your writing with a partner.

You will need:

computer with
Internet access,
reference books,
ruler,
paper,
pencil or pen

# Reach Higher!

## Write a Biography

- What famous person do you think is a good role model? Select a role model that you would like to learn more about.

- Copy the chart onto a sheet of paper. In the first column, write what you already know about the person. In the second column, write things that you want to learn about the person. In the last column, write information you find on the Internet or in reference books that answers your questions.

- Write a short biography about your person.

My role model _____

| What I Know | What I Want To Know | What I Learned |
|---|---|---|
| | | |
| | | |
| | | |
| | | |

# Challenge Yourself!

## People Making a Difference

- Suppose you were going to interview the role model you named in Reach Higher! Write a list of questions you would like to ask this person about his or her job. Include questions that help you learn about how this person helps others.

- Share your questions with a partner. Work together to create additional questions.

- If time permits, use the Internet and reference books to see if you can answer any of your questions.

# Interview a Classmate

**You will need:**
tape recorder/tape,
paper,
pencil or pen

## Get Started!

**1** Interview someone in your classroom. You may discover special things about that person you did not know.

**2** What do you already know about that person? What makes him or her special? Make a list of qualities you admire in that person. What would you like to know? Write a list of questions to ask him or her.

**3** Interview the person you choose. Make notes about his or her responses. Record the responses with a tape recorder. What did you learn about this person?

**4** Write the interview. Use a question-and-answer format. Share your interview with the person you wrote about.

You will need:

world map,
state map,
local map,
paper,
pencil or pen,
crayons or markers

# Reach Higher!

## Where in the World?

- Pretend you are a coin collector and want to collect coins from every country. With a partner, look at a world map. Write the names of as many countries as you can find in ten minutes.

- Now, on your own, make a list of the continents. Write the countries under the correct continent.

- Compare your list with your partner's. Did you write the same countries?

# Challenge Yourself!

## Make a Map

- What landmarks are famous in your state? Do you have mountains or a state park? Use a map to find the important landmarks in your state.

- Choose a landmark that you would like to go see. Make a map that shows how a person could get there.

- Label highways, towns, and other places or landmarks that would help a person find his or her way.

- When you have completed your map, write the directions for getting from your town to the landmark you chose.

# Give Me Directions

**You will need:**

paper,
pencil or pen,
crayons or markers

## Get Started!

In *Max's Words*, Max chose words to make a story and convinced his brothers to give him a stamp and a coin.

1. Now choose your words carefully to create a map of your classroom and write simple directions for how to get from the door to where you sit.

2. Label the important objects in the room, such as the chalkboard, windows, and the teacher's desk. Include a compass rose and a map key with important symbols.

3. Write the directions from the classroom door to where you sit. Be sure that your written directions and your map match.

4. Ask another student to check your written directions.

# Reach Higher!

## My Favorite Activities

- Think about two of your favorite activities. Make a Venn diagram. On one side, describe one activity; on the other side, describe the other activity. Where the circles overlap, describe how the two activities are alike.

- Use your Venn diagram to write two paragraphs describing the similarities and differences between your two favorite activities. Share your writing with a partner.

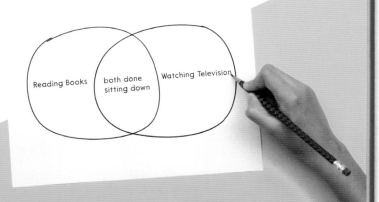

# Challenge Yourself!

## Compare Favorite Books

- Choose two of your favorite books or stories and make a Venn diagram about them. Describe the details of the books or stories. How are the characters, the setting, the main ideas, and the genres alike or different? Where the circles overlap, describe what they have in common. In the parts of the circles that do not overlap, write how each is different.

- Then write two paragraphs that tell how your favorite books are alike or different. Share your writing with a partner.

# Make a Book!

## Get Started!

1. What do you like to do for fun? Make a short picture book (about 4 pages long) telling about it.

2. Draw and color pictures that tell your story. You may wish to use short captions, speech bubbles, or sentences to explain the pictures.

3. Staple your pages to form the book and then add a book cover. Share your book with a small group of classmates.

# Reach Higher!

## A Fair Bargain

- What is your opinion of Grandpa Chon? Is the bargain he makes with Juan a fair one? Was Juan right to trust him?

- Write a paragraph comparing and contrasting Juan with Grandpa Chon. What do you think the two of them learn from each other in this story?

- Share your paragraph with your partner and other classmates.

# Challenge Yourself!

## Bird's-Eye View

- In *The Harvest Birds*, Juan gives credit to his friends, the zanate birds, for the success of his plan. What do you think the zanates think of Juan's success? Write a short story about the zanates and their role in what happened.

- If time permits, share your story with your class.

# Making Things Happen

**You will need:**

Student Book,
Context Cards,
paper,
pencil or pen

## Get Started!

1. With a partner, review *The Harvest Birds*. Use the Context Cards to review the vocabulary for the selection.

2. Suppose you knew Juan and wanted to encourage his dream to become a farmer. What would you say to him? Do you think it was hard for Juan to stay strong after the other people in the town laughed at him?

3. Write a friendly letter to Juan to show support. Use three of the vocabulary words in your letter.

4. Share your letter with your partner.

**You will need:**

Student Book,
Reading Log,
paper,
pencil or pen

# Reach Higher!

## Set in Japan

- Review *Kamishibai Man*.

- This story takes place in different settings in Japan. Describe how each setting looks and sounds and what it feels like. Using sentences and paragraphs, write your descriptions in your Reading Log.

- Share your writing with a partner.

# Challenge Yourself!

## What's the Theme?

- Think about the theme or message of *Kamishibai Man*. How does the main character teach a lesson? How does the author tell us his opinions about the changing world? Write notes in your Reading Log.

- Now write one or two paragraphs answering the above questions. Share your writing with a partner or small group.

# Read and Respond

## Get Started!

1. Reread the story of the *Kamishibai Man* with a partner.

2. As you reread, think about the following questions: What parts did you like the best? Why? How did you feel at the end of the story? Why? Where do you think the author got the idea for this story? What did you learn from this story?

3. Write notes about these questions in your Reading Log. Then write a paragraph to respond to the story.

**You will need:**

computer with
Internet access,
reference books,
paper,
pencil or pen,
crayons or markers

# Reach Higher!

### Edison's Ideas

- Use the Internet or reference books to learn more about Thomas Edison.

- What inventions used today are possible because of an invention by Thomas Edison? List the modern inventions that we would not have if it were not for this great inventor.

- Come up with an invention of the future that you think Thomas Edison might have invented if he were alive today. Write a plan for your invention.

# Challenge Yourself!

### How Does It Work?

- With a partner, choose one of Thomas Edison's inventions, such as the motion picture, light bulb, or phonograph.

- Look on the Internet or in reference books to discover how this invention works.

- Make and label a diagram to explain how the invention works. Share your diagram with the class.

# Modern Inventions

## Get Started!

1. In a small group, brainstorm a list of inventions that you and your family use every day in your home and in the classroom. Make a list of these inventions.

2. Sort the list of inventions into categories. The categories could be machines that entertain us, machines that help with household chores, or machines that are used for work.

3. Share your list with other groups.

Modern Inventions

**You will need:**

computer with
Internet access,
paper,
pencil or pen

# Reach Higher!

## Write a Biography

- Write a biography about Michael Jordan. Use the Internet to find information about him.

- Write your biography about either of these topics: Michael as a young boy or Michael as a professional basketball player.

- Draw pictures that support your biography. Add captions below each illustration. You may also wish to include a timeline.

- Think of a title for your biography. If time allows, present your biography to the class.

# Challenge Yourself!

## Be a Sportswriter

- Suppose you are a sportswriter attending an NBA (National Basketball Association) Finals game. Michael Jordan just made the game-winning shot to help his team, the Chicago Bulls, beat the Utah Jazz.

- Write a news article about the event. Include the five *W*s of news writing: *Who? What? When? Where?* and *Why?* (or *How?*). What was it like to watch the game surrounded by screaming, cheering fans?

- Share your writing with a partner.

# A Journal Entry

**You will need:**

paper,
pencil or pen

## Get Started!

1. Imagine that you are young Michael Jordan. You just played one-on-one basketball or "hoops" with your older brother Larry. Usually, Larry is the one who reaches higher, dunks the ball harder, and dribbles faster. Tonight, you beat your brother at his own game. How do you feel? Write a journal entry about it.

2. Write the journal entry as if you are the young basketball player. Describe how you feel after a game of basketball with your brother. Tell how playing with Larry pushes you to try harder. What are your dreams for the future?

3. If there is time, share your writing with a small group of classmates.

# Reach Higher!

## The Poetry of Science

Reread *Poems About Science*. Write a poem about how your life is affected by science.

- Think about some ordinary things you do each day. For example, you can turn on an electric light when you need to read or do homework. Write two things you do each day that science made possible for you to enjoy.

- Write a short poem about the effect of science on your life. Include the two ordinary things you wrote down.

- Write your poem on a sheet of paper. If there is time, share your poem with a partner.

# Challenge Yourself!

## Confidence Game

- In *The Science Fair*, Beany's friend Kevin always seems very confident. Write a paragraph on building confidence and self-esteem.

- Use library books and the Internet. Imagine that you are trying to help a friend become more confident. Choose four points you think are especially important for your friend to keep in mind.

- If time permits, read your paragraph to the class.

# Great Ideas

You will need:
Student Book,
paper,
pencil or pen

## Get Started!

**1** In the story *The Science Fair*, Beany is worried. She's afraid the project she and Kevin will present won't be good enough to beat the fancier experiments being planned by the other kids. Write a personal essay about a time you participated in a competition.

**2** Think of a time you were involved in a competition. It can be a sporting event, a science fair, or another kind of situation. Did you feel ready? Were you nervous? Write about how you prepared for the event.

**3** Share your essay with a friend. If time permits, compare experiences.

# Reach Higher!

## A Cherokee Leader

Sequoyah was a leader of the Cherokee people.
He developed a writing system so his people
and culture could be remembered forever.

- Use the Internet to research information
  about Sequoyah. Then write a biography
  about him. Explain why he was an
  important leader among the Cherokee
  people. Include a drawing of him and of
  the writing system that he developed.

- Share your biography with a small
  group of classmates.

# Challenge Yourself!

## History's Great Leaders

- Choose two great leaders from history that you admire. Use
  the Internet to research information about each leader.

- Write a news article that explains *who* the leaders were,
  *where* they lived, *when* they lived, *what* the greatest
  achievement of each was, and *why* they were good leaders.

- Display your news article so others can read it.

# Great Chiefs and Leaders

**You will need:**

Student Book,
paper,
pencil or pen,
crayons or markers,

## Get Started!

1. In the story *Yonder Mountain: A Cherokee Legend,* Chief Sky is too old to rule his people. He is looking for someone to become the next chief.

2. Write a book report about *Yonder Mountain.* Your summary should include the characters, setting, and problem. What action is taken to solve the problem? How does the story end? Tell why you liked or did not like this story.

3. Include an illustration of the story. If time allows, share your report with the class.

# Reach Higher!

**You will need:**

Student Book,
computer with
Internet access,
paper,
pencil or pen,
crayons or markers

## More to 4-H

- With a partner, review *Kids and Critters*. Then write a brief report on 4-H.

- Use the Internet to research 4-H. The programs mentioned in *Kids and Critters* are a small sample of the many ways 4-H helps young people. Choose a program not mentioned in the selection and write about it. Add a picture to illustrate.

- Share your report with a few other classmates.

# Challenge Yourself!

## A Day in the Life

- Write a story about a day in the life of a police dog.

- Review *Aero and Officer Mike* if you need to. Your story can be about Aero or another police dog. It can be about a day on duty, a training day, or a day when the dog visits a school or hospital.

- Share your story with another classmate. Draw a picture to illustrate your story if you wish.

# A Helpful Partner

**You will need:**

Student Book,
Reading Log,
pencil or pen

## Get Started!

1. With a partner, reread *Aero and Officer Mike*. Discuss the selection.

2. What did you and your partner think of the selection? Did you like it? What did you already know, if anything, about police dogs before you read the selection? What information was new to you?

3. Write about Aero and Officer Mike in your Reading Log. Do you think you would enjoy knowing them? What do you think of the kind of work they do? Share your writing with your partner.

# Reach Higher!

## Write a Recipe

- Think of your favorite meal.

- Now list the ingredients that you will need to make this meal.

- Write step-by-step directions of how you think you should prepare the recipe.

- When you have finished writing your recipe, look it up in a cookbook and compare it to the one you wrote.

# Challenge Yourself!

## Be a Poet

A *haiku* is a form of Japanese poetry that does not rhyme. It consists of three lines. There are five syllables in the first line, seven syllables in the second line, and five syllables in the last line.

- Write two haiku poems. Write one about a delicious food and one about a food that tastes yucky!

- Include adjectives to describe each food. Think about the mood you'd like to create with each poem, whether serious or humorous.

- Write a title for each poem. Then read your poems aloud to the class.

# You're the Chef!

**You will need:**

computer with
Internet access,
cookbooks,
paper,
pencil or pen,
crayons or markers

## Get Started!

1. Suppose you were the chef of a popular cooking show on TV. You are making a three-course meal that includes a salad, a main course with side dishes, and a dessert.

2. Create a menu made of healthful foods from these groups: the bread and grain group, the vegetable group, the fruit group, the milk group, and the meat and fish group.

3. Using cookbooks or the Internet, plan your menu.

4. Write a menu for the "Special of the Day" such as one you would see in a restaurant. Include a drawing that shows what your meal will look like when prepared.

Special of the Day

You will need:

recycled materials
to make puppets,
ruler,
art supplies,
paper,
pencil or pen

# Reach Higher!

## Reduce, Reuse, Recycle

- Whenever you reduce, reuse, and recycle, you are helping planet Earth. Think about *A Mr. Rubbish Mood*.

- With your partner, brainstorm a list of things that you can reduce use of, reuse, or recycle.

- Make a three-column chart. Use the headings *Reduce, Reuse,* and *Recycle.* Write the ways you can help our planet in the correct column. You may wish to draw pictures to go with your chart.

# Challenge Yourself!

## Puppets in the Spotlight

- With a partner, make puppets by reusing paper or other classroom materials.

- Then write a dialogue for the puppets telling how we can reduce, reuse, and recycle materials to help the environment.

- Share your puppets and dialogue with the class. Ask your classmates to think of other ways to reduce, reuse, and recycle materials.

# Save the Rainforests!

**You will need:**

computer with Internet access, world map/globe, paper, pencil or pen, crayons or markers

## Get Started!

1. Suppose you and your partner are scientists. You have been learning about what has been happening to rainforests around the world.

2. Using the Internet, research dangers to rainforests and what we can do to help protect them.

3. Write a paragraph explaining what is happening to the rainforests and how people can use these resources wisely.

4. With your partner, draw a map that shows where the rainforests are found worldwide.

You will need:

Student Book,
computer with
Internet access,
paper,
pencil or pen,
crayons or markers

# Reach Higher!

## Report a Discovery

Suppose you were a reporter who was with Barnum Brown
when he discovered the remains of a *Tyrannosaurus Rex* in 1902.
Review the story. Then write an article that includes:

• facts about the discovery;

• what Barnum Brown might
have said;

• and why this discovery can
help us learn about the past.

# Challenge Yourself!

## Write a Biography

• Write a biography of Barnum Brown,
the dinosaur hunter. Use the Internet
to find information and historic
photos of Barnum Brown.

• Draw a timeline that includes dates
and information about the
discoveries that he made.

• Display your biography where your
classmates can read it.

**Lesson 17**

# Report-a-saurus

**You will need:**

computer with
Internet access,
reference books,
paper,
pencil or pen,
crayons or markers

## Get Started!

1. Work with a small group. Use the Internet or reference books to find out more about an *Albertosaurus*.

2. Each group member should research one of the following topics: *Who discovered the* Albertosaurus? *Where were the fossils located? What did an* Albertosaurus *look like and eat? When did it live? What can the fossils tell us about creatures from the past?*

3. Together write a report and include information that answers each question. You may wish to draw a diagram of an *Albertosaurus*. If time allows, share your report with the class.

# Reach Higher!

## Make a Chart

- Review *Poems About Nature*. Choose a poem that reminded you most of a place you have been or would like to visit. On a sheet of paper, make a three-column chart. In the first column, write where you were or want to go. In the second, write what you know about the place now.

- In the third column, write what you might like to see or learn about this place. If you have been there, write something you would like to see or learn if you went back. Use reference books or the Internet to fill this column.

| where I went | what I know now | what I want to know |
|---|---|---|
|  |  |  |

**You will need:**

Student Book, computer with Internet access, reference books, construction paper, paper, pencil or pen, crayons or markers

# Challenge Yourself!

## Protect Trees

- Trees are a beautiful and important part of our world. Make a brochure for your classmates that tells them how they can protect trees.

- Use reference books and Internet sites, such as those for the National Parks Service or the Department of Agriculture, to get your information. Look for special tips and programs for kids.

- Make your brochure colorful and fun to read. Share it with your class.

# Did You Know?

**You will need:**

Student Book,
computer with
Internet access,
paper,
pencil or pen

## Get Started!

1. In the selection, *A Tree Is Growing,* you read some amazing facts about trees. Some of the facts were true for all trees. Others were true of particular trees only.

2. Review *A Tree Is Growing.* Choose one particular structure, shared by all trees, to write about, such as the leaves, sap, roots, or bark. Then choose a specific tree from the selection that has an interesting or unusual example of the structure you chose.

3. Write a brief paragraph using the facts you drew from the reading. If time permits, use the Internet to find other trees that have interesting examples of the structure you chose.

4. Display your paragraph in your classroom or share it with a partner.

# Reach Higher!

**You will need:**
Student Book,
tape recorder/tape,
paper,
pencil or pen,
crayons or markers

## Change the Story

- Suppose something prehistoric came from the volcano—like *Albertosaurus* or *Tyrannosaurus Rex*. How would Big Cheese and the mice rid Mousopolis of a giant dinosaur? What would a dinosaur be afraid of?

- Work with a group. Have someone begin telling the story. In turn, each person adds one sentence to the story. What happens? How does the story end? Record the story. Include the problem and solution in the story.

- Using the recorded story, write and illustrate a book about it.

# Challenge Yourself!

## Be a Movie Critic

- Suppose that you're a movie critic. *Dogzilla* is a film, and it is opening night.

- Write a review of the film. Is there an exciting chase scene, a funny scene, or a scary scene on an empty street in Mousopolis? Is the film serious, funny, or scary? Does the dialogue seem real? Tell about the costumes and set design in your review.

- Share your review with a classmate.

# Dogzilla: The Next Chapter

**You will need:**

paper,
pencil or pen

## Get Started!

1. Dogzilla never returned to Mousopolis but many puppies did arrive there from the volcano. Add another chapter called "Puppyzilla" to the selection *Dogzilla*. Are the mice surprised to see the puppies? What problems do the puppies bring?

2. Describe the setting and characters. What actions do the mice take to solve the new problem? Would Big Cheese lead the chase again? Could the mice "think like a puppy" to get the puppies to leave Mousopolis? How does the story end?

3. Begin your chapter where *Dogzilla* ended. If time allows, share your story with other members of the class.

# Reach Higher!

## Icy Climates

- What have you learned about the climate of the Arctic and Antarctic regions? What would you like to know? For example, do you know why temperatures in Antarctica are colder than in the Arctic? With a partner, write two questions you have about these regions.

- Work with a partner to find the answers to your questions by looking on the Internet, or in a science or reference book.

- Exchange questions and answers with other partners. List the new facts you learned.

# Challenge Yourself!

## Let It Snow!

Does it snow where you live? What causes it to snow or not to snow? When does it snow?

- Find out why it snows. Look up facts in a science book or an encyclopedia.

- Write a paragraph explaining what causes snow and why some regions of the world are much colder than others.

- What does snow remind you of? Compare snow to something you know and then draw a picture. For example, "Snow is like a blanket of soft white cotton."

# It's Cold Outside!

**You will need:**

Student Book,
index cards,
pencil or pen

## Get Started!

1. Work with a small group to create a game called "It's Cold Outside!" In this game, the questions are sentences or statements and the answers are given as questions.

2. Review *Life on the Ice* and write sentence clues on index cards that tell about something you have learned. For example: *Before 200 years ago, this continent was never before seen by human eyes.* On the other side of the card, write the answer in the form of a question: *What is Antarctica?*

3. When you're ready to play the game, place the clues in a pile. Divide your group into two teams. In turn, each team selects a sentence clue from the pile to ask the other team. Keep track of the number of correct answers each team has.

**You will need:**

Student Book,
ruler,
paper,
pencil or pen,
crayons or markers

# Reach Higher!

## Tiny Ants, Big World!

- Remember that the ants in the story think that common things are something else. Reread the story and then write a travel guide for ants.

- Label two columns with the headings: "What ants think it is," and "What it really is." Write ideas under each heading. You may want to add drawings.

- Share your travel guide for ants with the class if time allows.

# Challenge Yourself!

## Look Closely!

- Pretend you are a scientist who studies ants.

- Reread the story and think about what a scientist might observe the bad ants doing in the kitchen.

- Make a numbered list of the ants' actions in the order they happen. Share your list with another classmate.

# Write a Report

## Get Started!

**1** Reread *Two Bad Ants* and write a book report about the story.

**2** Include in your report the book title, the names of the author and illustrator, the characters, the setting of the story, and a short summary. Tell whether or not you liked the book and why.

**3** Design a cover for your book report. Display your report so others can read it.

# Reach Higher!

## Journey of the Whales

- Look at a map or globe. Find the Pacific coastline along which whales migrate.

- Choose one of the towns from which you might watch whales on their journey.

- Write a postcard to your family. Tell them why you would like to go to your chosen town to see whales migrate. Draw a picture of a whale on one side of the card. Write an address and draw a stamp on your postcard.

# Challenge Yourself!

## Write a Learning Log

- Using the Internet or other reference books, find out about why whales migrate, where they go, and how long it takes them to make the journey.

- Write a learning log, giving details on when the gray whale migrates, what it eats, and the time it takes to complete the migration. List your entries weekly. Be sure to include the date, time, and what was observed. Make sure your information is accurate.

- Display your learning log in your classroom.

# On Their Way

## Get Started!

Pretend you work for a newspaper. You write a newspaper column called "In the Garden."

 **1** Read this letter that has been sent to you by a reader:

> Dear Garden Helper,
>
> There are insects in my garden. How can I tell if they are grasshoppers or locusts?
>
> Sincerely,
> Son Flower

**2** Use the part of *The Journey: Stories of Migration* that tells about how grasshoppers and locusts look different. Then write a letter to answer the question above. Remember to include the important parts of a letter.

**3** Show a classmate pictures from the selection of a grasshopper and a locust. Ask him or her to read your letter and see if it correctly describes their differences.

# Reach Higher!

## Oliver's Visit

- Imagine that Oliver K. Woodman came to visit you.

- Think about the things you might show him. Make a list of these things.

- Choose one thing from your list and write a persuasive paragraph about why Oliver might especially like it.

# Challenge Yourself!

## A Special Stamp

The United States Postal Service has created many stamps to honor people. Among the people honored this way are "Pop" Warner, a football coach; Helen Keller, an advocate for people who have disabilities; and Philo T. Farnsworth, the inventor of the television.

- Think of a person you would like to see pictured on a stamp.

- Write a persuasive letter telling why you think this person deserves to be on a stamp.

- Make a drawing of your idea for how the stamp should look.

# Time for a Journey

## Get Started!

**1** Make a timeline of Oliver K. Woodman's journey across the United States.

**2** Put the dates and the places he stopped on the timeline.

**3** Add a date and a place he may have stopped in your town. Then write a letter to Tameka or Uncle Ray explaining the adventure Oliver had during his stay in your town.

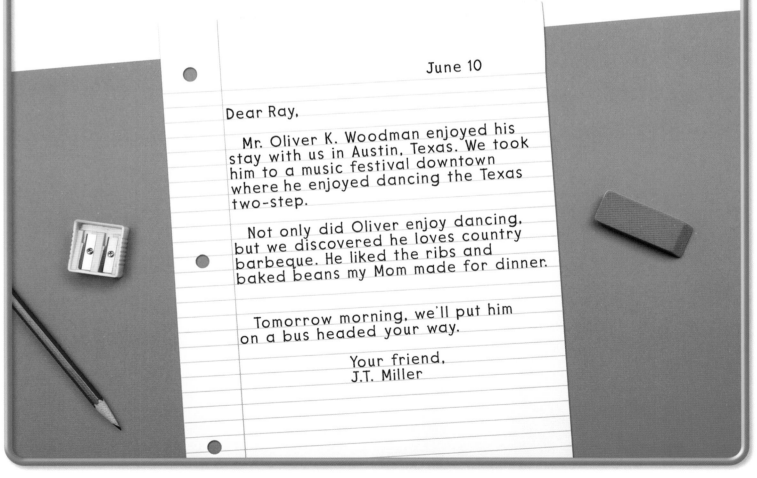

June 10

Dear Ray,

Mr. Oliver K. Woodman enjoyed his stay with us in Austin, Texas. We took him to a music festival downtown where he enjoyed dancing the Texas two-step.

Not only did Oliver enjoy dancing, but we discovered he loves country barbeque. He liked the ribs and baked beans my Mom made for dinner.

Tomorrow morning, we'll put him on a bus headed your way.

Your friend,
J.T. Miller

# Reach Higher!

## Why Is It Different?

- The Hawaiian monk seal is unique to Hawaii. Research the monk seal. Use an encyclopedia or the Internet to learn more about it.

- Write a paragraph about this seal. Tell what the monk seal eats, and where and how it lives. Write about what makes it different from other seals.

# Challenge Yourself!

## Hawaii's Plants and Animals

- Use an encyclopedia to find information about the plants and animals that live in Hawaii.

- Make a list of plants and animals that are found there. Tell whether these plants and animals are found only in Hawaii or if they are also found in other places in the world.

- Share your list with a partner. Which is your favorite animal or plant? Talk about it with your partner.

# Exercise for Good Health

**You will need:**

health books,
paper,
pencil or pen

## Get Started!

1. Think about the activities of the brothers in *Dog-of-the-Sea-Waves*. Think about how the brothers exercised when they swam, sailed, or fished. These activities helped keep their bodies healthy.

2. What activities help keep your body healthy? Use a health book to gather ideas. Make a list of these activities. Which of these activities do you do?

3. Show another classmate your list. Discuss the activities you listed. Ask him or her to add additional activities that keep the body healthy.

**You will need:**

Student Book,
computer with
Internet access,
paper,
pencil or pen,
crayons or markers

# Reach Higher!

## Who Will Reach the Top?

- Pretend that you are mountain climbers approaching the summit of a mountain. You and your partner both want to be first to reach the top.

- Prepare a short skit about mountain climbing. Present reasons why you should have the honor of being the first to climb to the summit.

- Present your skit to the class if time allows. Ask class members to decide who has the more persuasive argument.

- Use the Internet to find out how Hillary and Norgay answered the question of who reached the summit first.

# Challenge Yourself!

## Make a Catalog

- Think about the many items that mountain climbers need to carry. Some pieces of equipment are pictured in the story, but you can probably list several more.

- Prepare a "Mountaineers' Catalog." Include pictures and descriptions of items, such as cameras, tents, flashlights, and so forth. Use the information in *Mountains* to help you.

- Show your catalog to a group of classmates. Ask them which items they would want if they were mountain climbing.

# Interview an Explorer

**You will need:**
Student Book,
reference books,
paper,
pencil or pen

## Get Started!

1. Suppose you are a reporter. You and your partner are going to meet Temba Tsheri and interview him for a major magazine article about his climb of Mount Everest.

2. Reread *Mountains: Surviving on Mt. Everest* and then work with your partner to write questions that you wish to ask Mr. Tsheri.

3. Then try to find the answers to your questions in reference books. With your partner, present the interview to a small group. One of you acts as Mr. Tsheri while the other one asks the questions. Be prepared to answer additional questions the students may ask you.